SUPER CITIES!
T0047125
ALBUQUERQUE
ROUTE
66
by Michael Burgan

arcadia
CHILDREN'S BOOKS

**Published by Arcadia Children's Books**
A Division of Arcadia Publishing
Charleston, SC
www.arcadiapublishing.com



First published 2022

Manufactured in the United States.

ISBN 978-1-4671-9855-4

Library of Congress Control Number: 2021943254



Produced by Shoreline Publishing Group LLC
Santa Barbara, California
Designer: Patty Kelley

Contents

# WELCOME TO Albuquerque!

Can you think of an American city with a "q" in its name? How about a city with two?! The answer is **Albuquerque**! It's the largest city in the state of New Mexico, and it's also the state's city with the longest name.

Albuquerque isn't just a fun name to say, it's also a great place to live. Nearby mountains provide lots of outdoor activities, like hiking in the summer and skiing in the winter. The Rio Grande—"Big River" in English—is a favorite outdoor spot for fishing and kayaking

When play time is over, thousands of people work at the University of New Mexico in Albuquerque. Others work for high-tech companies and for the U.S. government in and around

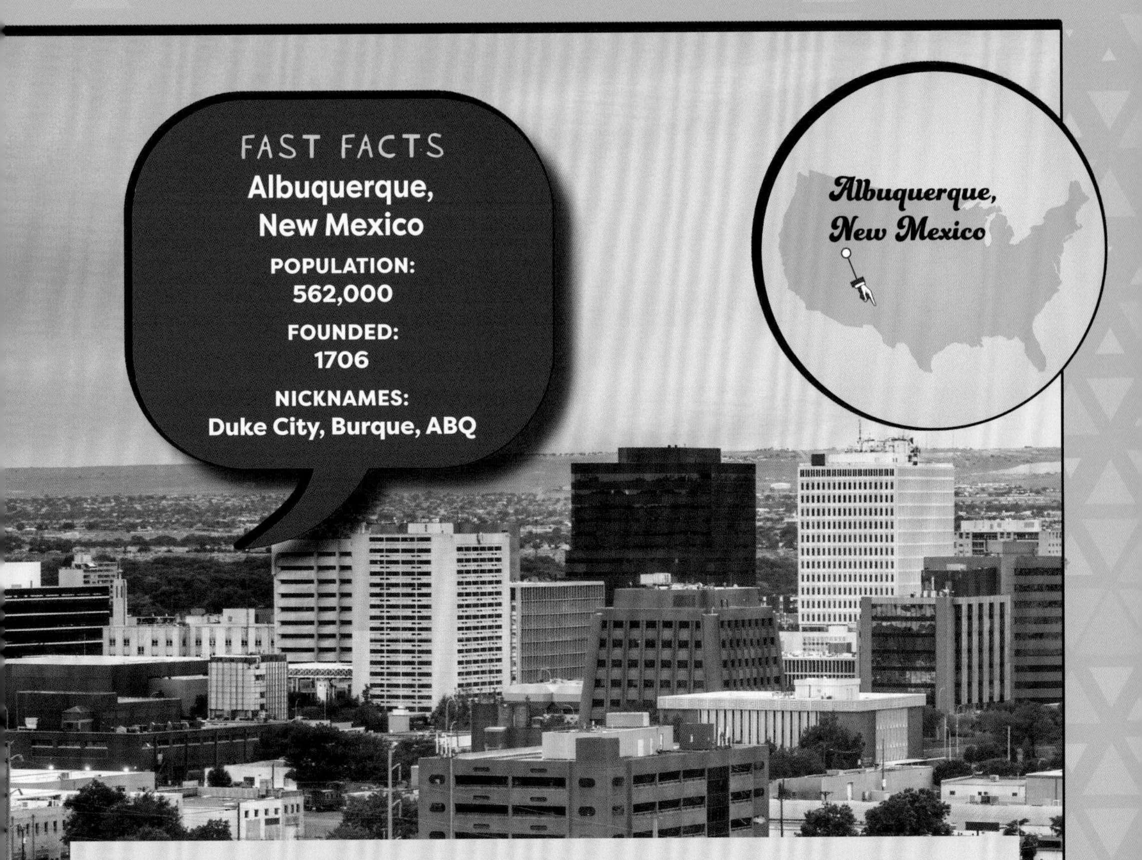


the city. These government employees range from Air Force pilots to scientists looking to use the wind and sun for energy. Speaking of sun—Albuquerque residents catch some rays about 300 days every year.

Like the rest of northern New Mexico, Native American, Latinx, and non-Latinx white people who trace their roots to Europe make up the majority of the population in this city. But the influence of other racial and ethnic groups—such as African American and Asian American peoples—helps create a distinctly blended culture. And the influence of Spanish and Mexican settlers on the city are always close at hand. ***¡Vaminos a Albuquerque!***

# ALBUQUERQUE: Map It!

To the east, Albuquerque is bordered by the Sandia and Manzano Mountains. The tallest peaks soar more than 10,000 feet high. Both names could make you hungry: *Sandia* is Spanish for "watermelon" and *manzano* means "apple tree." To the west of the city is a mesa—an elevated, flat stretch of land. Across Albuquerque, the elevation doesn't dip much below 5,000 feet, making it one of the highest major cities in the United States. The western edge of the city also has three volcanoes. They're known as the Three Sisters. Don't worry—they're dormant and don't blow their tops anymore.

Running through the city is the Rio Grande. The river provides water for a stretch of trees called a *bosque*—Spanish for "woods" or "forest." Cottonwood trees, which line the banks of the river, have grown in the bosque for more than one million years!

Just outside the city are several Native American pueblos, or villages. They have their own governments and invite the public to attend some of their ceremonies. These events are famous for their dances.

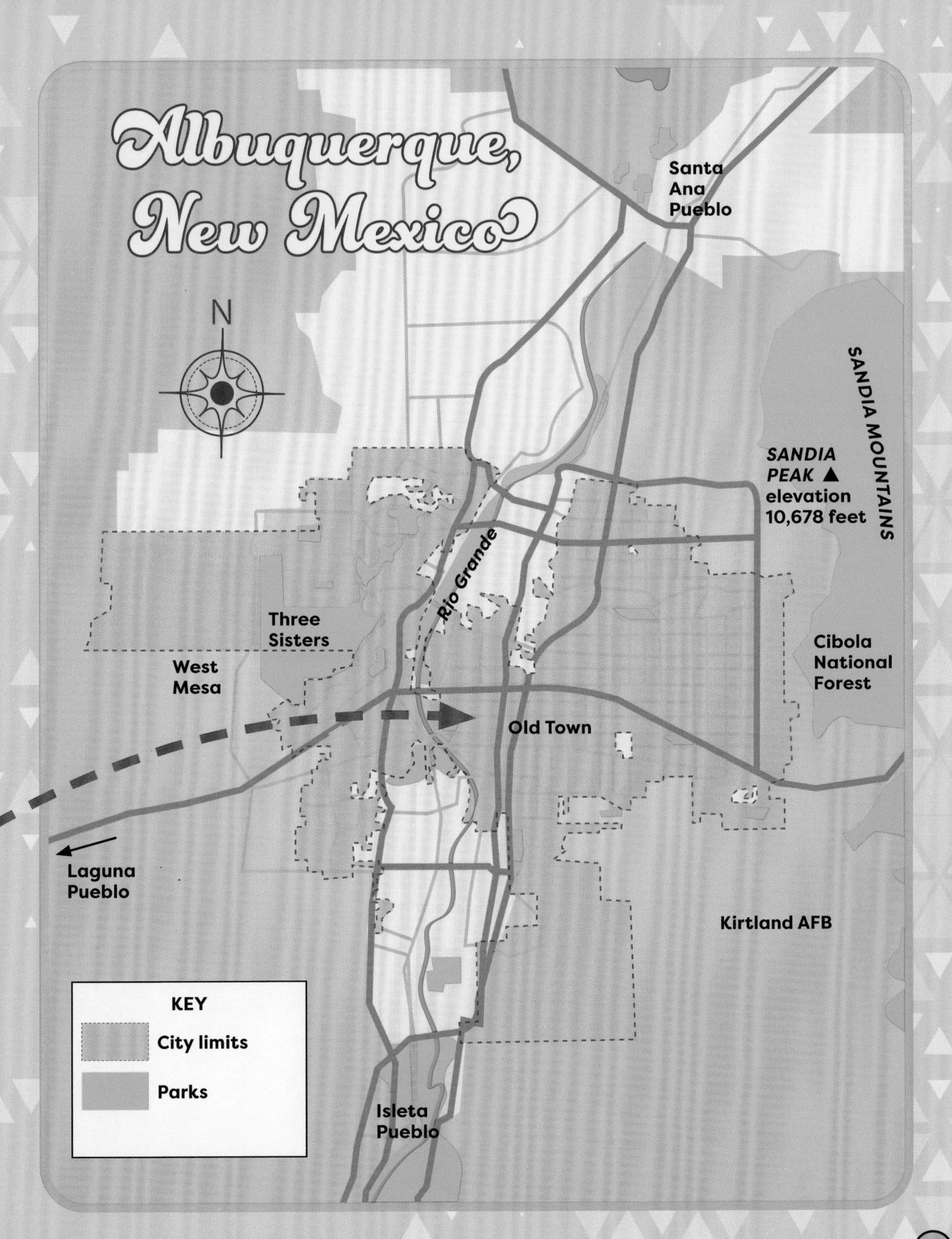
Albuquerque, New Mexico
N
Santa Ana Pueblo
SANDIA MOUNTAINS
SANDIA PEAK ▲ elevation 10,678 feet
Rio Grande
Three Sisters
West Mesa
Cibola National Forest
Old Town
Laguna Pueblo
Kirtland AFB
KEY
City limits
Parks
Isleta Pueblo

# Set the Scene

**Kirtland Air Force Base:** For more than 80 years, U.S. military planes have taken off and touched down at Kirtland Air Force Base. Kirtland covers a large part of southeastern Albuquerque. Air Force space research goes on there, too; they check out comets, stars, and planets.

**Sandia National Laboratories:** The scientists at Sandia tackle a range of issues. Some help design powerful weapons. Others help in the fight against diseases like COVID-19. Sandia has more than 12,000 people working in Albuquerque.

**Bosque:** To spot some of Albuquerque's wildlife, the bosque is the place to be. Birds, fish, and land animals of all kinds find a home in the trees and along the waters of the Rio Grande. Sixteen miles of trails let people enjoy the bosque, too.

**Sandia Peak:** Want to see all of Albuquerque at your feet? Head to Sandia Peak. You can drive up the east side of the mountain or take a tram that travels up almost three miles to reach the peak where you can get a great view of the city.

**Old Town:** Step back in time, sort of, in Albuquerque's Old Town. In 1706, Spanish settlers built a central open area here, called a plaza. Today, the east side of the plaza is home to local artisans, who sell everything from pottery to textiles to jewelry.

# ALBUQUERQUE MEANS . . .

The city is named for Don Francisco Fernández de la Cueva Enríquez, the 10th Duke of Alburquerque. At one point in the 1800s, the city dropped the first "r" in its name. Most folks today are just glad no one wanted to use Don Francisco's full name for the city! He was viceroy—sort of a like a governor—of New Spain, the name for lands owned by Spain in North America. He held that important position when Albuquerque was founded, so the settlers named their new town for him. And his title gives Albuquerque one of its nicknames—Duke City.

**Here's one view of the Duke . . .**

**. . . and here's another in his fancy go-to-war clothes.**

# BIG ON BALLOONS!

Visitors to Albuquerque can go up, up, and away in hot-air balloons that fly high over the city. The biggest attraction for balloon fans is the Albuquerque International Balloon Fiesta, held over nine days in the fall at Balloon Fiesta Park.

**It's the largest gathering of hot-air balloons in the world. About 500 balloonists bring balloons of all shapes and sizes to the park.**

**The biggest event of the fiesta is the Mass Ascension (that means "lift off"). All the balloons take off in waves!**

**Why Here?:** What makes Albuquerque such a hot spot for cool balloons? The winds! They create what's known as the Albuquerque Box. Cool air from the mountains settles in the Rio Grande Valley. The winds carry the balloons south. Then, winds from the other direction rise above that cool mountain air and push the balloons back where they started, letting the wind do all the work. After all, you can't steer a balloon!

**One event is the evening glow. After sunset, the burners that create the hot air needed to send the balloons aloft light up the evening sky.**

# ALBUQUERQUE'S PAST

The Pueblo people built multi-story buildings that are called pueblos (the word comes from the Spanish for "villages.") The building material was adobe—a mixture of mud and straw. Adobe bricks are still used in building today.

An example of ancient Pueblo pottery style.

The pueblos had rooms called kivas that were used for religious ceremonies. People entered some underground kivas by going down ladders.

People have been living in northern New Mexico for about 12,000 years. The ancestors of today's Pueblo people first lived in the Four Corners region—where New Mexico, Colorado, Utah, and Arizona meet. Around 1100, the people began to move southward and settle near the Rio Grande. A few centuries later, Native Americans who spoke a language called Tiwa started several pueblos near what is now Albuquerque. They raised corn, beans, melons, and other crops, while turkeys and deer provided some of their meat. Skilled craftspeople made pottery and jewelry, and weavers made clothes out of cotton, wild plants, and animal skins.

Most of the actual pueblos of the past no longer exist, but several survive around Albuquerque, such as Sandia, Santa Ana, Isleta, San Felipe, and Laguna. Also, there are 19 Pueblo tribes in northern New Mexico, and each is considered its own nation.

Some kivas and other buildings had artwork called murals painted on the walls. The murals often featured both animals and humans.

# THE SPANISH COLONY

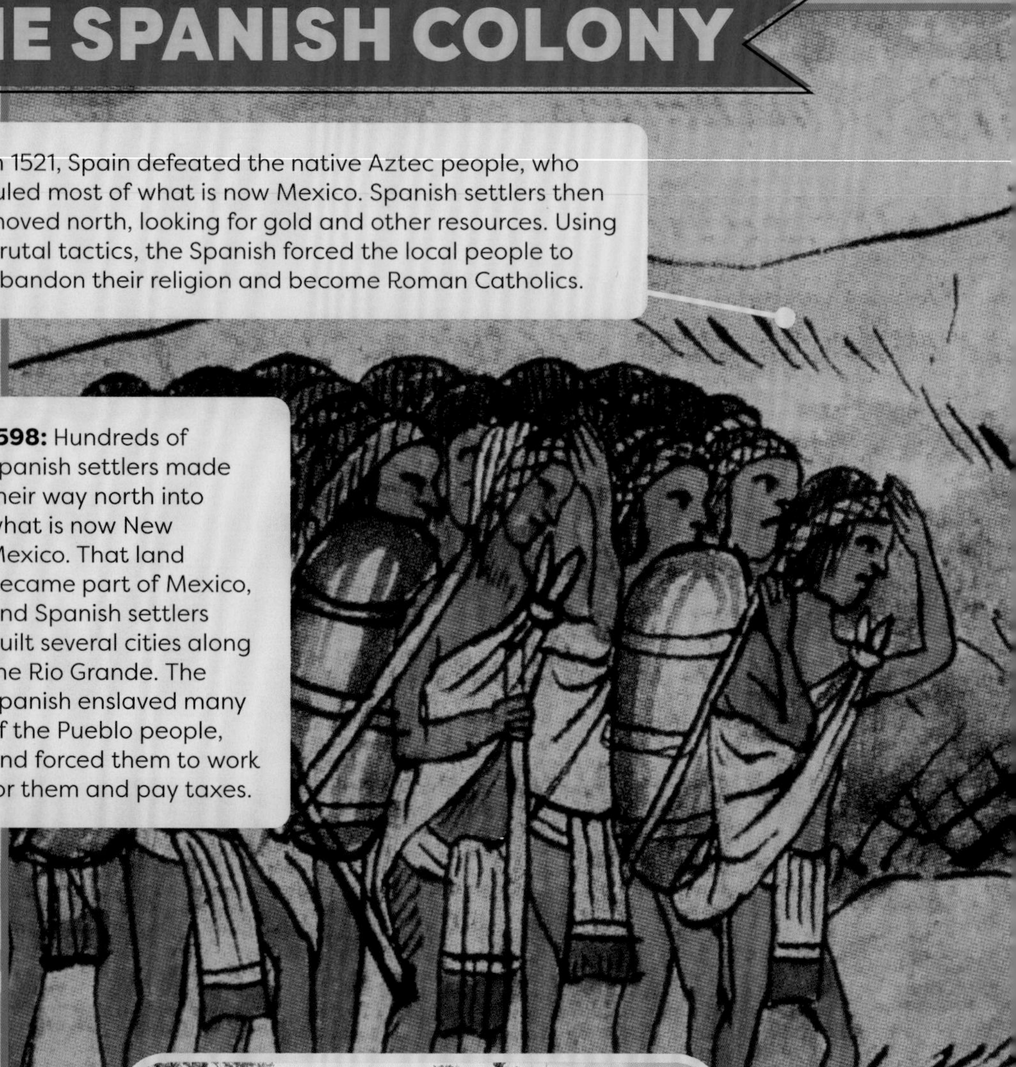

In 1521, Spain defeated the native Aztec people, who ruled most of what is now Mexico. Spanish settlers then moved north, looking for gold and other resources. Using brutal tactics, the Spanish forced the local people to abandon their religion and become Roman Catholics.

**1598:** Hundreds of Spanish settlers made their way north into what is now New Mexico. That land became part of Mexico, and Spanish settlers built several cities along the Rio Grande. The Spanish enslaved many of the Pueblo people, and forced them to work for them and pay taxes.

**At Aztec Ruins National Monument, remains of Pueblo Indian buildings can be seen.**

**1600s:** A few Spanish families farmed along the banks of the Rio Grande near what would become Albuquerque. But there was no town or village center.

**1706:** Several dozen Spanish families received permission to start a new town along the river. It was located about 60 miles south of Santa Fe, the capital of New Mexico. The settlers named the town Albuquerque.

The settlers created a plaza, or central square, and built a church and homes around it. The church was named for Saint Philip de Neri and was completed around 1719. The church also served as a kind of fort.

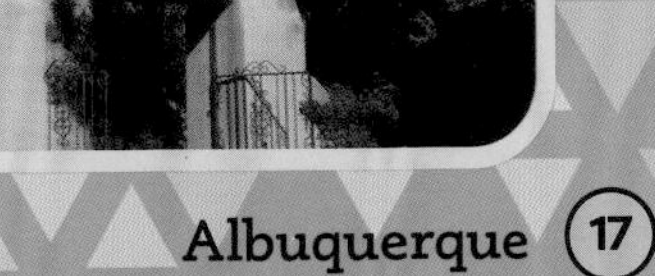

# INDEPENDENCE, BRIEFLY

As the 19th century began, a large part of the Mexican population was tired of being ruled by Spain. Starting in 1810, they began fighting a war for independence, just as American colonists did in 1775.

**1821:** Mexico won its independence from Spain. For the first time, the people of Albuquerque could legally do business with the United States. Americans came to the region to trap animals and trade.

**1846:** The United States wanted some of Mexico's land, and went to war to get it. The Mexican War ended in 1848, with the U.S. winning land that would become part of eight states, including New Mexico.

**1862:** During the Civil War, New Mexico was part of the North, or Union. Troops from Texas (which sided with the South, or Confederacy) briefly captured Albuquerque. But then a defeat outside of Santa Fe forced the Confederate invaders to leave.

**Hunters:** From colonial days into the 1800s, ciboleros, or "buffalo hunters," headed out from Albuquerque and nearby towns. They went to the plains of eastern New Mexico to track down the big, shaggy beasts. The buffalo—or bison—provided meat, hides, and fat that was used to make candles.

# A GROWING CITY

From 1706 on, most Burqueños, or residents of Albuquerque, were farmers. Some also sold wool from their sheep. But the city became a center for trade in New Mexico in 1880, when the first railroad reached Albuquerque. New businesses and homes sprung up near the tracks. This was the birth of New Town, while the original center near the plaza was named Old Town. Street cars pulled by mules connected the two parts of Albuquerque.

**1882:** The first balloon launched in the city soared more than 14,000 feet high. The city also got its first telephone service.

**1891**: Albuquerque had a population of just under 4,000.

**Early 1900s:** Albuquerque took over from Santa Fe as New Mexico's center for business. One big business was cutting and shipping lumber. Wool was an important product, along with clothing and items made from wool.

**1912:** New Mexico became the 47th U.S. state. Santa Fe became its capital city.

**1927:** Route 66, a highway that eventually ran from Chicago to Los Angeles, reached Albuquerque.

**1936:** In the middle of the Great Depression, New Mexico tried to draw tourists to the city. Many came to Albuquerque to learn about the area's Pueblo people and to explore its natural beauty.

**1941:** The United States entered World War II. Some businesses in Albuquerque began to make military equipment such as ammunition.

**1945:** The national laboratory known today as Sandia opened in the city.

**1961:** At 16 stories, the Bank of New Mexico headquarters became the tallest building in the city.

**1972:** The city hosted its first balloon fiesta, or festival.

**1975:** Bill Gates and Paul Allen started a software company called Microsoft. It later moved to Seattle and became one of the world's biggest companies.

# ALBUQUERQUE TODAY

What makes Albuquerque a favorite spot for residents and visitors today? Here are some of the things the city is best known for now.

**Natural Beauty:** The Rio Grande and the Sandia Mountains provide plenty of ways to enjoy nature, whether it's cycling on trails, hiking on paths, or skiing down slopes.

**High Tech:** Microsoft moved on, but the city still has plenty of companies that focus on computers, 3D printing, and other high-tech areas. Some of the work has ties to research done at Sandia National Laboratory and Kirtland Air Force Base.

**Movies:** Lights, camera, action! Well, it's not quite Hollywood yet, but filming TV shows and movies in and around Albuquerque has become big business! Netflix plans to spend several billion dollars to build studios and make movies there.

FAST FACT

A company owned by inventor Thomas Edison shot a short film about Pueblo school life in 1898 at the nearby Isleta Pueblo.

**Highway History:** As a famous song says, people have been getting their kicks on Route 66 for decades. It's been called America's Mother Road. Before the huge highways that we know today, Route 66 was the major roadway across the U.S. The longest stretch of Route 66 to still exist in any one city is along ABQ's Central Avenue.

**Food:** Albuquerque's food scene is big—and growing! Hispanic, Anglo, and Native American foods are often blended together, and ethnic foods from Africa and Asia add to the mix.

# City Builders

Here's a quick look at some of the people who helped make Albuquerque what it is today.

## Clyde Tingley

Clyde Tingley and his wife Carrie came to the city because she had a lung disease called tuberculosis. Albuquerque's warm, dry climate was thought to help people with the disease. Clyde became involved in local politics, and he helped build parks and pave streets. In 1934, he was elected governor of New Mexico. His friendship with President Franklin Roosevelt helped bring new building projects to Albuquerque and the state. They included buildings for the University of New Mexico.

## Alice K. Hoppes

The African American community makes up a small part of Albuquerque's population, but Alice K. Hoppes wanted to make sure they were never overlooked. For 12 years, she was the head of the city's chapter of the National Association for the Advancement of Colored People. In the 1980s, Hoppes also played a major role in making Martin Luther King Jr.'s birthday a state holiday.

### Francisco Cuervo y Valdez

There might not be an Albuquerque without Francisco Cuervo y Valdez. He took the lead in founding the city in 1706. Cuervo y Valdez was serving as the temporary governor of New Mexico at the time. He gave the settlement a very long name: Villa de Alburquerque de San Francicso Xavier del Bosque (and you thought "Albuquerque" was long!). Cuervo y Valdez spent most of his time as governor in Santa Fe. But the city he started remembers him with a statue in Old Town.

### Ben Abruzzo

Along with Maxie Anderson, Ben Abruzzo helped make Albuquerque the ballooning capital of the world. Abruzzo came to the city to serve at Kirtland Air Force Base. During the early 1970s, he and Anderson made some of the first hot-air balloon flights in the city. In 1977, the two made what was then the longest balloon flight ever—almost 3,000 miles from Maine to Iceland. The next year, they made the first balloon trip all the way across the Atlantic Ocean.

Albuquerque's Spanish and Mexican roots are strong. Today, almost half the city's residents identify as Latinx. But Albuquerque has also been shaped by the Pueblo nations and other Native American tribes. And the rich cultural traditions brought by the Black and Asian communities have all played a role in making Albuquerque what it is today. Who are today's Burqueños? Here's a look.

**Latinx Roots: Spain, Mexico, and More**

Spanish settlers from Mexico and New Mexico built Albuquerque. They brought their language, food, traditions, Roman Catholic faith, and more. Today Spanish is still widely spoken in the city, and some Spanish words are often mixed with English. Roman Catholic churches are still easy to find in Albuquerque—there are more than two dozen of them.

In recent decades, new Latinx immigrants have settled in Albuquerque. Many come from Mexico, while others are from Central and South America. For three days, October 31-November 2, many Burqueños with Latinx roots celebrate Día de los Muertos—the Day of the Dead. It's a time to remember and honor friends and relatives who have died.

**Native Americans**

The Pueblo Indians built their villages along both banks of the Rio Grande near what is now Albuquerque. Several of these pueblos remain. In colonial days, some Native Americans and Spanish people married, and some people in and around Albuquerque still carry that mixed heritage. Today, some Pueblo people work at the pueblos, while others live and work in Albuquerque itself. The city also has residents who trace their roots to other peoples of the Southwest, such as the Navajo, Apache, and Zuni (below). Overall, people from several hundred tribes live in the city!

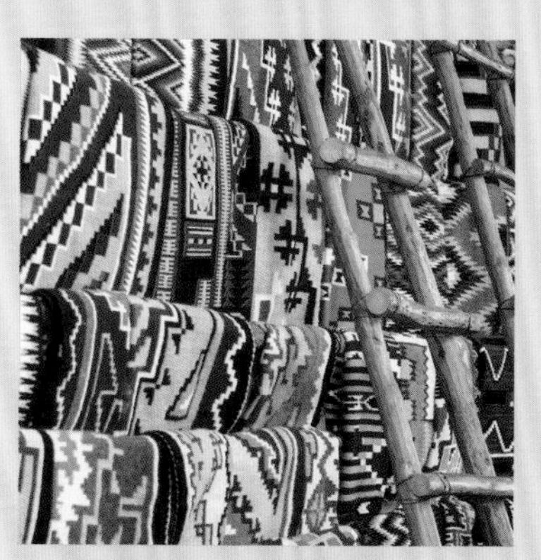

FAST FACT

**Among U.S. cities, Albuquerque has the sixth-largest Native American population.**

**Europeans**

After New Mexico became a U.S. territory, white Americans began to head west to settle there. So did immigrants from all over Europe. Their homelands included Germany, Italy, Greece, and the United Kingdom. Many of the newcomers found their way to Albuquerque. Some started businesses and built homes in the city. Many immigrants found work in the railyards or on farms. People of many different backgrounds still play important roles in Albuquerque's economy and government.

**This restaurant's name was inspired by early American city settlers.**

### African American Community

The African American community in New Mexico can trace its roots back hundreds of years. After the Civil War, thousands of Black men became "buffalo soldiers" in all-black units of the U.S. Army. Those soldiers helped keep the peace as the U.S. expanded west. As formerly enslaved men and women traveled into the Albuquerque area, they built homes and churches and started businesses. It wasn't easy—like elsewhere in the U.S., Black families constantly faced discrimination and unfair treatment. But the rich cultural traditions of the Black community have deep roots in Albuquerque, and continue to grow.

**A performer at one of ABQ's many cultural festivals.**

### The Asian Influence

The first immigrants from China and Japan began to arrive in the Albuquerque area in the late 1800s, most working on the transcontinental railroad, or stopping on their way to California to look for gold. More than 100 years later, families from other southeast Asian nations—especially Vietnam and the Philippines—began to arrive and contribute to Albuquerque's rich diversity. Despite city-wide racial discrimination, many Asian communities supported one another as they built homes and started businesses. Today Asian-owned shops, restaurants, and cultural centers are an integral part of the Duke City.

**Lunar New Year decorations in Albuquerque.**

# Hot and Dry—and Getting Drier

## Albuquerque Climate and Weather

Albuquerque lies in the Chihuahuan Desert. On average, it gets less than 10 inches of rain each year. That rain usually falls in the summertime. The city gets other water from melting snow in the nearby mountains. The temperature in these dry deserts are often quite high.

What does higher heat mean for Albuquerque? Its famous river can sometimes run dry. The Rio Grande is sometimes called the "Rio Sand" south of the city. Portions of the river dry up during the summer. But in 2021, the sandy stretches popped up farther north in Albuquerque, too. That means no water for kayakers—and for the fish that call the river home. To save water, city residents can only water outdoor plants on certain days during the spring and summer.

FAST FACTS

**Climate means what the weather is like over long periods of time each year. Weather means what it's like outside right now!**

**When to Visit**

As you've seen, Albuquerque can be hot, especially in the summer. July and August can also be rainy. Storms called monsoons can blow in and then blow out almost every day. Spring can bring strong winds that create dust storms. And tumbleweeds really do tumble across the streets! Fall is an ideal time to visit—the days are still warm, but not too hot, and the nights cool off. Winter days are nice, too. The city gets about 10 inches of snow each year, but rarely all at once. More snow falls in the mountains.

# Albuquerque Was My Home

**Linda Chavez**
***Writer and Politician***

Linda Chavez can claim family roots in New Mexico that go back several centuries. One of her distant relatives was governor of New Mexico while it was part of Mexico. Chavez was born and raised in Albuquerque but left the city to go to college. She became active in politics and worked under President Ronald Reagan on the U.S. Civil Rights Commission. Chavez is also a writer—she has written several books and many newspaper articles.

**Ralph Bunche**
***Diplomat and Peacemaker***

The Bunche family moved to Albuquerque when Ralph was a teenager. He only spent a few years there, but he's honored in the city for his legacy of work. Bunche studied politics and worked for the U.S. government. In 1948 and 1949, he worked to help end conflict between the Arab people of Palestine and the people of Israel. He won the Nobel Peace Prize in 1950. He was the first African American to win that high honor.

**Rudolfo Anaya**

If you grew up in New Mexico, chances are you read the novel *Bless Me, Ultima* (1972). Rudolfo Anaya's book blends the state's Spanish and Native American history. It's considered a classic of Latinx literature. Anaya was born in a small New Mexican village but moved to Albuquerque as a teen and later taught in the city. His works, published through his death in 2020, also included poetry and children's books.

**Jeff Bezos**

***Entrepreneur***

You may have heard of a little company called Amazon and its founder, Jeff Bezos, one of the richest people in the world. But did you know Bezos was born in Albuquerque? That's where his mother met Bezos's adoptive father, who was a Cuban immigrant. The family left the city when Bezos was still a boy. After he attended college and worked for several companies, he started Amazon in 1995 in Seattle—in his garage!

400-E
ART
TAFOYA
GALLERY
FLUTES
HAND MADE
JEWELRY
OPEN

# Things to see in Albuquerque

Tourist time! If you're a Burqueño, you (probably) know all about these places. But if you're visiting, here are some sights you'll want to see. Plus, check out the section on museums later in this book!

## Old Town

The heart of old Albuquerque is a hopping place! Visitors come to shop, eat, and get a taste of what the city was like three centuries ago. Here are some of the favorite spots.

## Serving Up Science

Calling all science geeks and tech nerds! Just on the edge of Old Town is Explora. This hands-on science center lets kids—and their adult friends—learn about gravity (what goes up, must come down), electricity (sure to give you a jolt), and so much more.

## Holy Ground

The current Church of San Philip de Neri was finished in 1793. It features thick adobe walls, which help keep out the summer heat and the winter chill. It's one of many old adobe buildings that line the plaza at the heart of Old Town.

## Rock On!

You don't always have to go to a museum to see art. Petroglyph National Monument features centuries-old art carved into rocks by Native American people and Spanish settlers. (*Petroglyph* means "old rock carving.") The monument has more than 25,000 carvings, including all kinds of animals, people, and handprints left by the artists. And some of the images puzzle art experts, who don't know exactly what they're supposed to be.

## Peak Viewing

The best place to see all of Albuquerque is at Sandia Peak. And the best way to get there, is the tramway. Board the tram for a soaring 15-minute trip that takes you more than 10,000 feet above sea level. Get your camera phones ready! At the top, you have an incredible view. And if you're hungry, there's a restaurant there, too.

## Where Tribal Nations Meet

Duke City is home to the largest gathering of Native American peoples in North America. The Gathering of Nations Powwow takes place over the last weekend in April. Singers and dancers from more than 700 tribal nations compete for prizes. The event also features a market and plenty of Native American foods.

## One Wild Museum

On the other side of Sandia Peak, just outside of town, is a museum like no other. It's called Tinkertown, and it's the work of Ross Ward. He was a wood carver who settled in New Mexico and wanted to show off his work. He eventually built a 22-room museum with 50,000 glass bottles and other junk items cemented into the walls. Tinkertown features items from the Old West, mechanical games, and Ward's carvings.

Locals agree that Albuquerque's sunny weather and natural wonders make for great outdoor activities. Here are some of the places where you can explore outdoors.

## Valle de Oro National Wildlife Refuge

This place is for the birds—and other wildlife, too! The U.S. government took an old dairy farm along the Rio Grande and is turning it into a home for more than 570 species of birds. This protected land is one of the few wildlife refuges located in a U.S. city.

**Golden-fronted woodpecker.**

FAST FACT

**The nature center is located in what's called a flyway—a path that many birds follow as they migrate (travel) from one place to another. Think of it as a bird highway!**

## Rio Grande Nature Center State Park

Here's another spot close to the river where you can hike and see all sorts of birds. More than 250 different kinds of feathered creatures live or

visit here. Panels called blinds let you watch the birds like roadrunners, juncos, and doves without them seeing you, so you don't scare them off. From the blinds, you might also spot turtles sunning themselves in between dips in a pond.

## Elena Gallegos Open Space

Get a view of the Sandia Mountains and surrounding area from this open space. It sits about 1,000 feet above the main part of the city. It's a treat to eat outdoors here. The space has covered picnic tables to keep out the sun, and some of the tables have grills, too.

## La Luz Trail

Forget the tramway or a car—you can use foot power to reach the top of Sandia Peak on this trail. La Luz cuts back and forth in what are called switchbacks to get from the city to the mountain top. It's about an eight-mile hike. You'll see plenty of wildflowers along the way.

# ABQ BioPark

It's a zoo, it's an aquarium, it's a botanic garden, it's all that, and more! The ABQ BioPark has something for everyone. Here's what you'll find in one of the state's most popular tourist spots.

**Zoo:** The BioPark's zoo has been bringing the animal kingdom to Albuquerque for almost 100 years. About 250 different species call the zoo home, including polar bear and snow leopards, along with penguins and a new spot just for animals native to Asia. Don't miss the capybara. Weighing in at 120 pounds, it's the world's largest rodent.

**Botanic Garden:** Stop and smell the roses—and other flowers—at BioPark's Botanic Garden. More than 1.5 miles of trails wind their way through several gardens. There's also the BUGarium, with dozens and dozens of species of insects, arachnids, and other creepy crawlies. The garden has a building that houses about 40 different species of butterflies, moths, and bees too.

**Tingley Beach:** Fishing, not surfing, is what draws most folks to Tingley Beach, named for one of Albuquerque's past mayors (see page 24). The "beach" is actually several ponds. Some visitors sail model boats on the water. Others come to have picnics or look at the wild animals that live on or near the ponds.

**Aquarium:** There's nothing fishy about it—this is the place to see hundreds of sea creatures! The aquarium brings water dwellers like stingrays, tarpon, and jellyfish to the desert. Sharks of all sizes are among the attractions here. And the aquarium is not just about fish. You can see different kinds of sea turtles, sea birds, and even an otter.

# GETTING AROUND ALBUQUERQUE

With so many things to do and see, people in ABQ need ways to get around. Albuquerque has the usual buses, taxis, and ride shares. Here are some other local options.

**Train 1 : Some folks roll into town on the train. Amtrak, the nation's passenger rail service, makes a stop. The train passes through ABQ on its way to or from Chicago and Los Angeles.**

**Train 2: If you're looking for another way out of the city, you can ride the rails on the Rail Runner. This train cuts through several pueblos as it chugs north to Santa Fe. Mostly, it brings workers back and forth between the cities.**

**Bus:** Once you leave your plane or train, how do you get around? Well, Albuquerque has a bus system that covers the city. Along Central Avenue, some special buses only make a few stops, making it faster to get from point A to point B (or even C!).

**Bikes:** Albuquerque is spread out, so most residents have cars. But some choose to use pedal power to get around. The city has more than 400 miles of bike trails and paths. And if you want to go off road in the summer, Sandia Peak has 30 miles of trails. Going up is hard work, but just imagine that fast ride down!

# IT'S OFFICIAL!

Cities like to name "official" things. That basically just means that lots of people who live there like something! Here are some of Albuquerque's "official" city things.

FAST FACT

**New Mexico is the only state with an official question— "Red or Green?" meaning what color chile do you want on your food.**

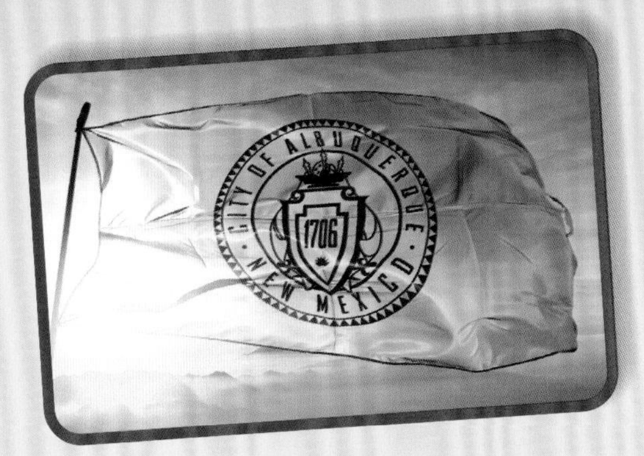


### OFFICIAL CITY FLAG AND LOGO:

The center of the logo features a symbol called a Zia. It has a circle with four sets of lines coming from the center. The lines represent the four directions of east, west, north, and south. They also stand for the four seasons and four times of day— morning, noon, evening, and night. The symbol was first used by the people of Zia Pueblo. And the upper left corner shows a bird in flight. The city flag (below left), like the logo, has the year 1706, the year Albuquerque was founded, in the center.

**OFFICIAL CITY TREE:**
Desert willow, a flowering tree native to the Southwest

Welcome to NEW MEXICO Land of Enchantment

## OFFICIAL NEW MEXICO STATE STUFF

**Nickname:**
Land of Enchantment

**Amphibian:**
New Mexico spadefoot toad

**Bird:**
Greater roadrunner

**Fish:**
Rio Grande cutthroat trout

**Insect:**
Tarantula hawk wasp

**Mammal:**
American black bear

**Reptile:**
New Mexico whiptail lizard

**Car Art:** One infamous piece of Albuquerque public art is a giant sculpture that artist Barbara Grygutis created by putting a car (yes, an entire car!) atop a large arch; she then covered the whole thing in blue tiles. Grygutis named her creation *Cruising San Mateo I*, but Burqueños call it *Chevy on a Stick*.

Outside museums and galleries, you can find great outdoor art in the heart of Albuquerque. The city has a program that puts art in public spots—there are more than 1,000 sculptures and murals around town. There's even a real car sitting on an arch. Another sculpture is made from dozens of car doors that look like feathers—it's called AutoHawk.

## Outdoor Art

Here are more examples of the city's art. For art that you can see indoors, turn the page for more details.

**Stone Rattlesnakes:** Where can you see not one, but two, 200-foot-long rattlesnakes? Head just south of the Sunport and you'll spot 'em. They're not real—thank goodness! These rattlers are made out of cobblestone.

**Botanical Mural Project:** You don't have to head to BioPark's gardens to see native plants. If you wander through downtown, look out for murals by the Argentinian artist Pastel, who has painted murals of flowers on some of the buildings.

When it gets too hot, you can always go inside to find great art. Here are some of Albuquerque's major art museums.

**Casa San Ysidro:** This house just outside Albuquerque is part of the Albuquerque Museum. It's also called the Gutiérrez/Minge House, the names of the folks who built it around 1875. They were its last private owners. Inside are artworks and crafts from Pueblo, Navajo, and Hopi artists, along with the work of Latinx woodworkers and weavers that date back to the 19th century.

**Albuquerque Museum of Art and History:** A little history, a little art—this museum has it all. The art part includes 10,000 items. Many of them show the influence of Pueblo and Spanish culture. There's Native American jewelry and pottery, too, along with paintings from artists who started moving to the state in the early part of the 1900s.

**University of New Mexico Museums:** Along with books and classrooms, UNM also has four museums. Its art museum has prints, paintings, photos, and sculptures, some of them hundreds of years old. And if you're a rock hound, head over to the school's Geology Museum. It's filled with rocks, gems, and minerals. To see a real rock star, check out the Meteorite Museum (above). A meteorite is a rock that zipped through space and landed on Earth. The meteorite here weighs one ton!

**Harwood Art Center:** The center provides space to artists of all kinds. More than 30 artists call this their creative "home." Twice a year, people can come in and see what the artists have created. Visitors can do more than see art here—they can make it, too! The center offers classes to kids and adults. You could make a papier-maché head or your own animated film.

Art is just the start when it comes to museums. You can explore many more in Albuquerque.

**Unser Racing Museum:** It's a vroom with a view! The Unser family settled in Albuquerque, and brothers Al and Bobby won fame as two of the best race-car drivers in the world. Between them, the brothers won the Indianapolis 500 seven times. Al's son Al Jr. (below) carried on the winning ways, winning "Indy" three times. Some of the family's cars are on display at the museum. You can also learn about racing history, and even take a spin in a virtual race car.

**Turquoise Museum:** This is one gem of a museum. J. C. Zachary once owned a turquoise mine. He loved that blue-and-green rock so much that he created a whole museum for it! Here in one of the world's hotspots for turquoise—several mines are still active in New Mexico—you can see one of the world's largest collections of the stuff. You can also see how the raw rock is turned into jewelry.

**Anderson-Abruzzo Albuquerque International Balloon Museum:** If you like a slightly slower ride, this museum is for you. It's named for Maxie Anderson and Ben Abruzzo, record-setting balloonists from Albuquerque. (See page 25.) The museum is packed with facts about ballooning history and science. Find out how those giant balloons stay in the air.

**Holocaust and Intolerance Museum of New Mexico:** This museum is dedicated to ending hate and intolerance through education. The exhibits—made up of artifacts, pictures, documents, videos, and books—teach visitors about historical conflicts caused by local, national, and global prejudice, especially the Holocaust. The Holocaust happened during WWII, when German Nazis killed more than 6 million European Jews. The act of killing whole populations based on their ethnicity, religion, or race is called genocide. It is still happening around the world today, and the NMHM aims to provide knowledge about genocide, intolerance, human rights, and social justice issues everywhere.

We're not done yet! Here's where you can explore science and the stars.

**New Mexico Natural History and Science Museum:** Dinosaurs once roamed New Mexico. You can see fossils of their ancient bones at this museum. They include some from a *Seismosaurus*, which—at more than 100 feet long—shook the ground 150 million years ago!

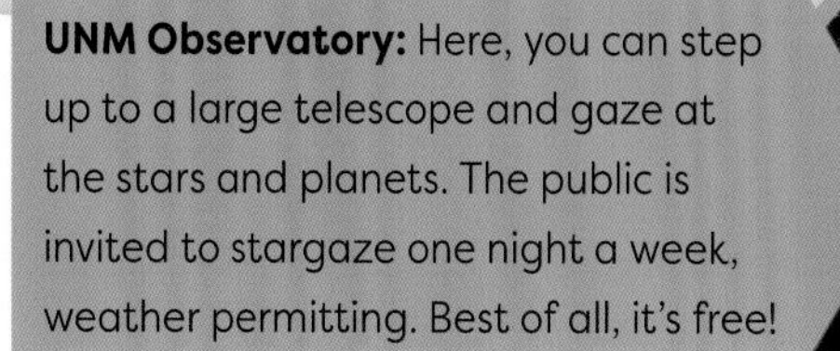

**UNM Observatory:** Here, you can step up to a large telescope and gaze at the stars and planets. The public is invited to stargaze one night a week, weather permitting. Best of all, it's free!

**National Museum of Nuclear Science and History:** During World War II, scientists working in Los Alamos, New Mexico, created a new weapon—an atomic bomb. It was the most powerful bomb ever made, and was used to end WWII. This museum explores nuclear science, which led to the creation of these weapons. Nuclear missiles like this one are also on display. Nuclear power has peaceful uses, too. It can generate energy for cities and keep ships and submarines at sea for months at a time, with no need to refuel.

**The American International Rattlesnake Museum:** Those huge stone snakes near the Sunport aren't the only rattlers in Albuquerque. Old Town is home to the American International Rattlesnake Museum. It houses the largest collection of live rattlers in the world! Learn about their venomous bite, which can be deadly.

FAST FACT

**The Rattlesnake Museum has another poisonous critter on display—a gila monster named Mollie that likes to eat small rats.**

For the really big shows, Burqueños head just a bit out of town to the **Isleta Amphitheater**. This outdoor arena is named for a nearby Pueblo.

There's more live music, dance, and drama in store at **Popejoy Hall**. It's on the UNM campus and holds almost 2,000 people. The school has several smaller theaters, too.

If you like live music, dance, and stage shows, Albuquerque has you covered! Here are some of the performing arts you can see.

There are three big stages at the **National Hispanic Cultural Center**. They host everything from plays, dance shows, and movies to concerts and puppet shows. The center's mission is to showcase Hispanic arts, past and present, from around the world.

When big-name comedians come to town, they get plenty of laughs at the Kiva Auditorium. Musical acts play the Kiva, too. It's just one part of the **Albuquerque Convention Center**, where large rooms also host shows (right).

# How to Talk Like a Burqueño

Some words and sayings only make sense to the people who live in a particular place or city. Here are some things you might hear folks in Albuquerque say.

## Christmas

**Sure, everyone knows what Christmas is, but in Albuquerque it also helps you pick dinner. When you're asked in a restaurant if you want red or green chile on your food, say "Christmas" to mean you want a little of both!**

## LUMINARIA

**Speaking of Christmas, when the holiday comes, some folks place small candles in paper bags filled with sand. These luminarias are then used to decorate walkways and adobe walls.**

# The Big I

**Near the center of the city, two major highways cross each other. Interstate 25 goes north-south through the city, while I-40 goes east-west. The Big I is where the two roads meet.**

## *Bueno bye*

**Bueno is Spanish for "good," so this is just the Albuquerque way to say goodbye.**

## ¿Que no?

**Here's another bit of Spanish. *Que no* is spoken as a question at the end of sentence and means, "Right?" Pretty neat, *¿que no?***

# ALBUQUERQUE'S Weird Side!

Who are you calling weird? Maybe we should just say some things are a little . . . different in Albuquerque. Here are some examples:

Here's the point—lots of folks love the giant red arrow stuck in the ground outside Indian Plaza shopping center. A construction business used a red arrow as its logo. In 1961, it put up this enormous arrow outside some stores it built. About 20 years later, some people wanted to remove it, but fans of the arrow shot down that idea.

Most volcanoes shoot out scorching hot lava. Not the one in the Duke City. It shoots out water! It's part of the city's efforts to control the flow of water after sudden, heavy rains. The volcano is made of lava rocks and stones. Water runs under the volcano then shoots out the top. The water then flows downs the sides, just like lava pouring out of a real volcano.

What's a snowless snowman? One made out of tumbleweeds! Each year just before Thanksgiving, some government workers gather up some of the dried balls of weeds. The tumbleweeds are then formed into a "snow"man that can reach 14 feet tall! Cars passing by on I-40 can admire this desert holiday tradition. Other nearby towns build tumbleweed Christmas trees.

Where's the world's largest structure made just from wood and glue? You guessed it—in ABQ. The ATLAS-I testing platform was built on Kirtland Air Force Base to carry out special tests on warplanes. It's 1,000 feet long and 600 feet high. It's not used today, and visitors can't get on the base to see it. But you can catch a glimpse of it from some spots in the Sandia Mountains.

# What People Do IN ALBUQUERQUE

What do people do for work in Albuquerque? As in other cities, they own shops, work in offices, and provide all sorts of essential services. But these are some of the really popular types of work that keep tens of thousands of people busy.

**Government:** Both the state and national governments have offices in Albuquerque. And of course, the city needs workers to keep Albuquerque humming. But the places that really put people to work are Kirtland Air Force Base and Sandia National Laboratories.

**Health:** The state's largest hospitals are in Albuquerque. They provide thousands of jobs to doctors, nurses, and all the staff that keep New Mexicans healthy. There are smaller medical clinics, too.

**Tourism:** Plenty of folks hit the road and head to Albuquerque—about 6 million each year! These tourists spend lots of dough while they enjoy the city. That money means tax dollars for the government and jobs for tens of thousands of Burqueños.

**Education:** The University of New Mexico has more than 15,000 employees, though some are located outside the city. They need that many because the college educates about 90,000 students! The city of Albuquerque also employs about 12,000 teachers and staff for K–12 schools.

# Hey! I'm from Albuquerque too!

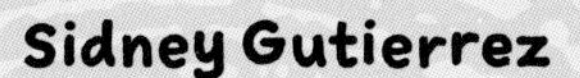


In 1985, Sidney Gutierrez made history when he became the first Latinx American to become a NASA astronaut. He left his hometown of ABQ to join the Air Force in 1969. He flew as a test pilot and taught others to fly. As an astronaut, Gutierrez spent more than 20 days in space on two space shuttle missions. After his high-flying days, Gutierrez led a private company that built rockets used to launch satellites into space.

### Notah Begay III

This Albuquerque native is one of the few Native American people to ever win a professional golf tournament. Begay traces his family roots to the Navajo nation and the Isleta and San Felipe Pueblo nations. He was a teammate of golf great Tiger Woods in college. Today, Begay reports on golf for TV networks. In 2005, he started an organization to help Native American kids get involved in sports.

### Lauren Sanchez

If anyone knows news, it's Lauren Sanchez. She left her hometown of Albuquerque to work in television news in Los Angeles. After a stop in Phoenix, she covered sports for the Fox Network. Back in Los Angeles in 2013, Sanchez won an Emmy Award for her work. That's a big deal—an Emmy is the most important award in U.S. television.

# Eat the Albuquerque Way

There's plenty of good food to chow down when you visit Albuquerque. Here are some local favorites.

**Sopapilla:** These doughy desserts are made of wheat and puff up when they're fried in oil. At the end of a meal, they're usually served with honey. But at some Albuquerque restaurants, you can start your day with a sopapilla stuffed with eggs and other breakfast goodies.

**Contain Yourself!:** Take a trip around the world, food-style, at Green Jeans Food Hall. Pairs of old shipping containers have been stacked together to create this foody paradise. Coffee, pizza, tacos, Asian food—you can have it all in one spot! A similar spot called Tin Can Alley opened in 2021.

ALBUQUERQUE GREEN JEANS FOOD HALL

**A Taste of Pueblo Cooking:** The restaurant inside the Indian Pueblo Cultural Center is just one of the spots in town that features food with a Native American flair. Some common ingredients in Pueblo cooking include blue corn, piñon (pine) nuts, bison meat, and beans.

FAST FACT

**Some Native Americans in Albuquerque bake in traditional ovens called *hornos*. They're made of adobe and look like giant beehives. Spanish settlers first brought them to the region.**

**What We Eat From New Mexico**

**Green chile * Pistachios * Pecans * Milk * Cheese * Onions * Beef**

# Eat the Heat

When people think of local food in Albuquerque, they think of chiles. This kind of pepper can really have some pop when it comes to spicy heat, but there are mild chiles, too. Green chile forms the basis of sauces and stews, but red chiles are also used. Green and red chile sauces can go over enchiladas, burritos, tamales, and all sorts of other foods with roots in Mexico. One local favorite is a green chile cheeseburger. Some restaurants compete each year at the state fair in Albuquerque to claim the crown of green chile cheeseburger champ.

These chiles aren't burnt. They're roasted! You can eat these right off the grill, or mix into dishes of all kinds.

# CHILE FACTS

**What is a ristra?** These strings of dried chiles are used as decoration in New Mexican homes. Sometimes people make Christmas wreaths out of chiles!

**Why are they different colors?** It's the same plant (actually a fruit, not a vegetable!). Green chiles have not ripened as long; red chiles stayed on the vine longer.

**Why New Mexico?** Chiles have been grown in the Americas for thousands of years. New Mexico locals found that the plants grew very well in the hot, dry weather. Spanish explorers took the chiles back to Europe, and today the plants spice up meals around the world. New Mexico is the biggest chile producer in the United States.

# Taking the Field!

Albuquerque doesn't have any teams in the country's major sports leagues. But that doesn't mean there are no fun and games. Here are teams that call the city home.

## ALBUQUERQUE ISOTOPES

Play ball! That's what the Isotopes do in their stadium near the UNM campus. The 'Topes, as they're called, play in the Triple A-West league. That's one of baseball's minor leagues just below the Majors. The Isotopes help develop players for the Colorado Rockies. The team's name refers to atoms found in chemicals and marks Albuquerque's role as a center for science. The team first took the field in 2003. Several years before that, the city had a Triple A team called the Albuquerque Dukes. Some big-league players who once played for the Dukes include Hall of Famers Pedro Martinez and Mike Piazza.

## NEW MEXICO UNITED

Albuquerque sports fans get a real kick out of the United. The team plays in the United Soccer League (USL) Championship division. Overall, the USL is the largest soccer league in North America. The United draws fans from around the state to watch its games, which are played at Isotopes Park. And it draws players from around the world, including Germany, Greece, and Uganda, along with the good ol' USA.

NEW MEXICO
UNITED
18

## DUKE CITY GLADIATORS

These Gladiators don't have swords and shields—just some pads and their football skills. But football played indoors? You bet, and the Gladiators are darn good at it. In 2018 and 2019, they won the Champions Indoor Football league championship. They play in the Indoor Football League now. Teams play on a field half the size of a National Football League field, with eight players on each side. Many of the rules are the same ones used in the NFL and college football. Most years, the Gladiators play at Tingley Coliseum, which is located on the state fairgrounds.

## NEW MEXICO ICE WOLVES

The puck stops here! To find hockey in the high desert, check out the New Mexico Ice Wolves. The Wolves joined the North American Hockey League in 2019. The players are still perfecting their skills—most are still in their teens! The best will move on to the big time, in the National Hockey League.

## ELEVATED ROLLER DERBY

Things really get rockin' and rollin' when the Elevated take the track! This roller derby team is part of the Women's Flat Track Derby Association. One skater on each team tries to roll past the opposing players to score points. The women on the team play for fun, not money. Albuquerque has had a team since 2005.

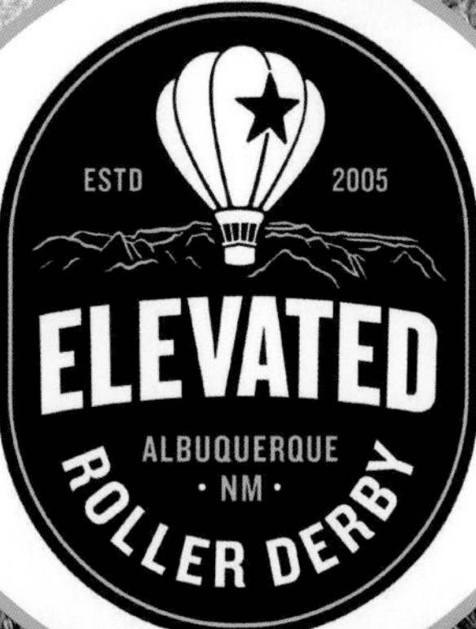

# Other Sports!

Burqueños don't just watch sports. They have plenty of ways to stay active year-round.

The city has several **golf courses**. The best of the bunch may be the one on the UNM campus. If you just want to practice your swing, two of the city-owned courses have driving ranges. Several of the area pueblos also get into the swing of things with their own courses.

Get get ready to explore the **50-Mile Activity Loop**. This loop of trails, roads, and bike lanes circles the city. Walkers, runners, and cyclists can use any part of the loop. The bike lanes include special sections that limit car speeds to just 18 miles per hour for bikers' safety.

If you're a master of moguls, **Sandia Peak Ski Area** offers wintertime fun. It has 300 acres of runs. Anyone from beginners to experts can find a trail just right for them. Snowboarders can enjoy the slope, too. And soon, the ski area hopes to have a coaster ride that snakes down the mountain when there's no snow.

**Rock Climbing/Hiking**: With so many rocks and mountains nearby, it's no wonder that people like to climb them! Sandia Mountains Foothill Open Space, Jemez Wilderness, Box Canyon, and El Rito are popular spots for beginners or experts. Locals can practice by climbing on special walls at indoor gyms.

# COLLEGE TOWN

How smart is this—residents from across New Mexico head to Albuquerque to earn college degrees. Here are some of the schools they attend.

## UNIVERSITY OF NEW MEXICO

**Founded** 1889
**Students:** 20,000
**Popular majors:** health professions, business, psychology, biological and biomedical sciences, education
**Fast Fact:** The UNM campus is the home of the Pit, a sports arena dug 37 feet into the ground. The school's basketball teams play there, and the Pit has also hosted concerts and the Gathering of Nations Powwow.

LOBOS

## CENTRAL NEW MEXICO COMMUNITY COLLEGE (CNM)

CNM
Central New Mexico Community College

**Founded** 1964
**Students**: 23,000
**Popular majors:** liberal arts and sciences, general studies and humanities, health professions, business
**Fast Fact:** CNM has six campuses spread across Albuquerque and one in neighboring Rio Rancho.

## CARRINGTON COLLEGE

**Founded** 1967
**Students:** 350
**Popular majors:** nursing, dental assisting, massage therapy, medical billing and coding, pharmacy technology
**Fast Fact:** Carrington College is a private school with campuses in seven states, including New Mexico.

## SOUTHWESTERN INDIAN POLYTECHNIC INSTITUTE

**Founded** 1971
**Students:** 370
**Popular majors:** liberal arts and humanities, business, culinary art, drafting and design, medical technician
**Fast Fact:** Students at the institute come from more than 120 Native American tribal nations.

# LOL!

## Albuquerque Riddles

Go ahead and laugh at Albuquerque—its people won't mind! Here are some riddles to tickle your funny bone.

**Why are Balloon Fiesta tickets so expensive?**

The prices can go UP every year!

**What happens when you bury an "S" in the middle of the desert?**

It turns into dessert!

**Which museum gets the most glowing reviews?**

The National Museum of Nuclear Science & History!

**How can you get cold in Albuquerque?**

Eat a lot of "chillys."

**What do New Mexicans eat for Thanksgiving?**

Albu-turkey!

**What is the most fang-tastic museum in Albuquerque?**

The Rattlesnake Museum!

# It's Alive! Animals in Albuquerque

You know what's wild? All the different kinds of animals that call a big city like Albuquerque their home. You can find wildlife in the mountains and the bosque—and even in neighborhoods! Here are some of the critters you might spot.

Black bears

Rabbits

Porcupines

Bobcats

Raccoons

## Night Howls

What's that howling on a New Mexico night? It's probably a coyote. These relatives of wolves are found all across the United States. But they have a special place in the folk stories and religious beliefs of Pueblo people and the other Native peoples of New Mexico. In one tale, the coyote is outsmarted by a bird. The bird sets out a stone that looks like it. The coyote tries to eat the stone, and it ends up losing all its teeth!

# It's Alive! Animals in Albuquerque

Albuquerque wildlife also finds homes in and around waterways. And when you look up in the sky, you can spot some of the flying critters that live in the region.

Desert tortoise

Turkey vulture

Pintail duck (there are 19 species of ducks that live in or visit New Mexico)

Collared lizard

Bald eagle

## Meep! Meep!

You learned a bit about the coyote. Now it's the roadrunner's turn. It's more than a famous cartoon character. New Mexico's state bird is often seen in and around Albuquerque. What makes it so special? Well, a roadrunner can sprint past a running person. And it can catch and kill a rattlesnake. Roadrunners also chow down on lizards and scorpions.

It's not always easy being a wild animal in a big city. You have to dodge cars, humans, and maybe bigger animals. Here are two organizations in the Albuquerque area that try to help injured critters.

## Wildlife West Nature Park

This park is just outside the city, in Edgewood. Injured animals from all over New Mexico are brought here so they can heal. For one reason or another, they can't be released back into the wild. So, they stay at the park, where visitors can come see them. The animals here include owls, hawks, coyotes, bears, raccoons, and elk. The park covers more than 120 acres, so there's plenty of room for the nature park to also hold events of all kinds. In the past, events have included kite-flying festivals and fairs about farming.

## Wildlife Rescue of New Mexico

Wildlife Rescue is in the heart of the city, inside the Rio Grande Nature Center State Park (see page 38). This group treats injured animals, too. But the goal here is to get the animals healthy enough to go back into the wild. Another goal is to educate New Mexicans about how humans can be a threat to wildlife. Pollution and putting up buildings where wild animals live can kill the critters.

## Save the Mouse!

Protecting animal habitats is really important, especially if the animals are endangered. *Endangered* means their species could go extinct (which means to disappear forever)! One Albuquerque native that's endangered is the New Mexico meadow jumping mouse. They love water—and they can jump up to three feet.

# Spooky Sites

Do you believe in ghosts and spirits? Not everyone does . . . but no one knows for sure! Like most cities, Albuquerque has some buildings that people say are haunted.

A trip to the movies didn't go well for Bobby Darnell. Back in 1951, the six-year-old went to see a film at the **KiMo Theater**. A water heater blew up, and the explosion killed poor Bobby. Now, folks say he haunts the theater, which is used today mostly for concerts.

Old Town is known for its history—and one slightly scary ghost! A figure called the Lady in Black has been seen in the **Chapel of Our Lady of Guadalupe**. People have heard the ghostly figure praying—and sobbing!

In the legend of **La Llorona**, a woman became angry at her husband and took it out on her kids—by throwing them in the river. When she realized what she had done, La Llorona began to cry—and has been crying since! Her wailing can be heard along the Rio Grande River. Some locals call her the ditch witch!

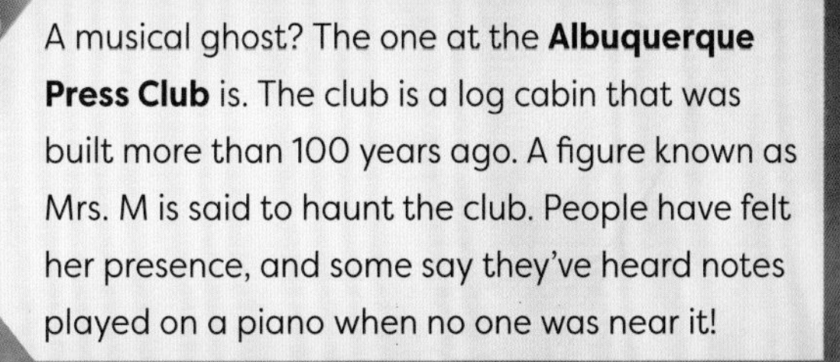

A musical ghost? The one at the **Albuquerque Press Club** is. The club is a log cabin that was built more than 100 years ago. A figure known as Mrs. M is said to haunt the club. People have felt her presence, and some say they've heard notes played on a piano when no one was near it!

The hotel **Parq Central** was once a hospital for people with both mental and physical illnesses. In the old days, patients said they saw objects move by themselves or heard spooky voices when no one was around. Today's hotel guests insist that ghosts still check in.

# Not Far Away

Whether you live in Albuquerque or come for a visit, you'll find other awesome places that are close by. Get a driver and hit the road for these sights outside the city.

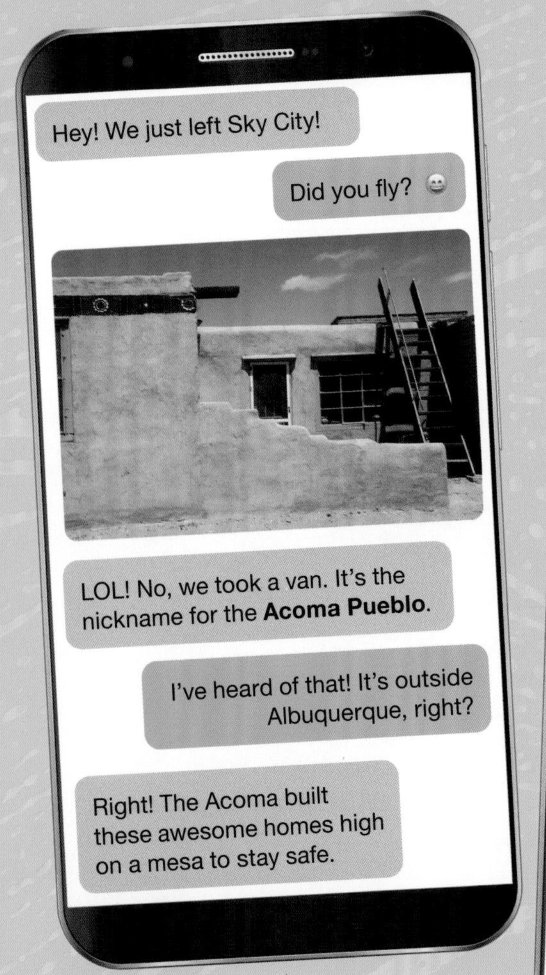

Trivia time!
Bring it on, quizmaster!
Where did Walt Disney get one of his best ideas for Disneyland?
From a mouse!
Bzzz! Nope! He saw the Christmas lights in **Madrid, New Mexico**. It was a big mining town and had a famous display every December.
Madrid like in Spain?
No, they say MAH-drid.
That's like saying Mex-IK-oh! 😁
This Madrid is on the **Turquoise Trail**, a beautiful road off of I-125.
Bueno!

# Not Far Away

## Santa Fe: Capital City

For another trip out of Albuquerque, head north to Santa Fe. That's New Mexico's capital city! At about 7,000 feet above sea level, Santa Fe is the highest capital city in the country (take that, "mile-high" Denver!). It also has the oldest government building in the United States. The Palace of the Governors was built in 1610 and is now part of the New Mexico History Museum.

If you're in Santa Fe, a stop at the **farmers' market** is a must. The smell of roasting green chile fills the air, as farmers from all around the region sell a wide range of food, from fruits and veggies to bison meat.

One of the oldest adobe buildings in Santa Fe is **San Miguel Chapel**, which was built around 1610. Its giant bell was made in Spain in 1356. Below is the San Miguel's chapel to Our Lady of Guadalupe.

Santa Fe is known for its art. The paintings of one of New Mexico's greatest artists—**Georgia O'Keeffe**—fill the museum that bears her name. O'Keeffe is famous for her sweeping landscapes and paintings that feature flowers and animal skeletons. One of her works sold in 2014 for more than $44 million—that's the highest price ever paid for a painting by a woman artist.

# Sister Cities Around the World

Did you know cities can have sisters? Why not brothers? Well, that's just what they're called. Sister Cities was started in 1956 as a program of the U.S. government. The idea was to connect cities here and around the world to help people get to know each other. Today, Albuquerque has 10 "sisters" around the world!

**Sister Cities in Action**

Here are some examples of how Albuquerque is working with and helping its sister cities:

**Chihuahua:** Chihuahua is the capital of the Mexican state with the same name. Many New Mexico residents from Mexico come from the state of Chihuahua. The two sister cities signed an agreement in 2019 to share ideas about policing, universities, and business.

**Ashgabat:** When this city celebrated the 140th anniversary of its founding in 2021, some Burqueños joined the party. A video "birthday card" featured a singer from Albuquerque performing a song written just for Ashgabat and sung in the Turkmen language.

**Sasebo:** The relationship between Albuquerque and Sasebo began when individuals from both cities met and became friends during the Korean War. Since the two have become sister cities, they've had several student exchanges. Some 85 students have gone to Japan or New Mexico.

**Helmstedt:** This sister city has also taken part in student exchanges with Albuquerque. The two have also sent groups of adults to each other, so they can learn more about the culture and history.

Books, Websites, and More!

## Books

Biggers, Ashley M. ***100 Things to Do in Albuquerque Before You Die.*** St. Louis: Reedy Press, 2018.

Burgan, Michael. ***New Mexico.*** New York: Children's Press, 2018.

Dean, Jessa. ***The Ghostly Tales of Albuquerque (Spooky America).*** Charleston: Arcadia Children's Books, 2021.

Hayes, Amy. ***Native Peoples of the Southwest.*** New York: Gareth Stevens Publishing, 2017.

Laine, Don, and Barbara Laine. ***Frommer's Easy Guide to Santa Fe, Taos, and Albuquerque.*** New York: Frommer Media, 2020.

# Web Sites

***Visit Albuquerque***
https://www.visitalbuquerque.org/

***City of Albuquerque***
https://www.cabq.gov/

***Albuquerque International Balloon Fiesta***
https://balloonfiesta.com/

***Indian Pueblo Cultural Center***
https://indianpueblo.org/

***National Hispanic Cultural Center***
https://www.nhccnm.org/

***12 Best Places to Go with Kids in the Albuquerque Area***
https://www.tripsavvy.com/where-to-take-kids-in-albuquerque-57568

# Photo Credits and Thanks

Photos from Dreamstime, Shutterstock, or Wikimedia unless otherwise noted. Alamy: 16: Agefotostock; 58L: Richard Ellis. Newscom: 69T: Hank Gutknecht/Zuma Press. 70: AP Photos: Adolphe Pierre-Louis/ Albuquerque Journal.

Artwork: LemonadePixel. Maps (6-7): Jessica Nevins.

Thanks to our pal Nancy Ellwood, Kait Leggett, and the fine folks at Arcadia!

# INDEX



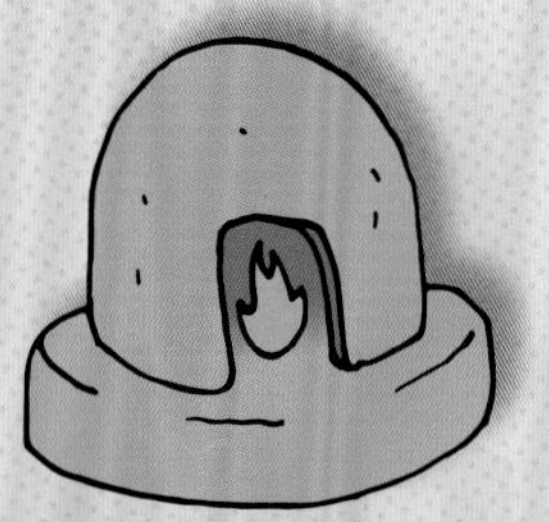